Read my Story, Hear God's Glory:

Read my Story, Hear God's Glory:

A Healing Journey

Krystal A. Hughes

I would like to first give all praise to the one and only God I serve and revere, Jesus Christ. I thank him for all he has done for me and for trusting me to write this book to you. I also want to thank the beautiful people in my life that support me daily, not only through this journey, but in life.

Thank You in no particular order,

Nicole Daniels, Tomica Daniels, Jammie Davis, Cheyenne Flood, Kameisha Pitts, Diandria Hughes (Nikki), Naamonde Lega, Angel McGuire, Naterria Mosely (RIP), Shenita Lawson, Freada Hughes, The Rock City Church.

To you All, I am most grateful and I couldn't imagine life, this book, and many more things to come without your unwavering, Love, Support and Encouragement. I also promise to do the same and all areas of your life.

Thank you also to these people, who have supported me at sometime in my life and I am grateful for ever crossing paths with,

Robert Bryant, Ricky Cheatham, Kendall Nancy, Velma Jones, Asbury United Methodist Church.

DEDICATION

CONTENTS

CONTENTS

Preface

"Heal" is a trending word we see and hear everywhere, especially following traumas and surrounding mental health talks. These days we even see it being thrown around as insults online when people say, "Go heal!" Or "Who hurt you!" The trend is just that: a trend, a hot topic word, or a speaking point, but those of us that have truly gone through and are on the other side of healing can honestly say there's power in that word and in that action. I am writing this book because I remember crying out in my darkest moment for help, and even though I did have some form of help, I did not feel like healing was taking place or I necessarily had the proper tools to heal. I was wondering why my church was not helping; I wondered why my close family and friends' supportive words weren't enough. I even wondered why God was not saying anything (this was the toughest one to swallow). I wallowed, wondered, and fought until I realized that healing was a choice and action that only I was in charge of. Now, the above things I mentioned were very important on my healing journey, but it was still up to ME to heal. This book is for everybody who has been through anything, and I do mean anything that makes them see themselves differently, handle themselves differently, handle other people differently, hurt themselves or others, make you lose hope, or send you into spaces you've never seen yourself in, do things you've never done (drugs, one-night stands, etc.), make you turn your back on God, make you hate yourself, your life, others, anything that alters who you truly are, this book is for you. My friend, I wrote this book for you because I have also experienced (another trending word) TRAUMA. Trauma will make all those things I just listed appear normal and just a part of life when life truly does not have to be lived like this. Life is for the living, and nothing on that list is positive, peaceful, productive, or powerful. In other words, it's a pitiful life to live.

In this book, I will walk you through a few of my traumas (childhood trauma, abandonment, a murder case, trying to find a job with a record, rape, family trauma), what they made me feel like and what things I was displaying during each trauma. Maybe you can identify yourself in my actions/feelings, even if you can't identify yourself in the exact trauma I went through.

I will also tell you what tools I used to get to where I am now, in a healed space. Thriving, not only back to my old self, but to a NEW person, with the restoration of everything I lost and much more. I can only attribute all of the healing and restoration to the one and only true God I serve, Jesus Christ. Even with that said, God alone is not enough to heal totally, and He put forth more things and people on this Earth to aid us. He has all the power, but He still used other people, the disciples, prophets, and much more to save, restore and teach in the bible. He left some of those same things here with us, starting with Yourself.

1

Childhood Trauma

I would like to say that I was born very well aware, but that would make no sense because I had to learn something from somewhere. I just hate to admit that most of my learning has been through some form of trauma. One of my earliest childhood memories is my father cutting my uncle with a razor blade so brutally that the scar that remains looks like he had open heart surgery. I was only maybe four or five years old and the only witness. I cannot recall feelings or understanding then, but I can attest to the strife it made between my family and even between my uncle and us later in life. The next memory I have from there was around my seventh year when my mom decided to leave my two younger sisters and me in the back of her suburban flatbed truck to go party with her friends at an old club back in Birmingham, AL, named the Brass Key. As we lay there, alone and admittedly scared, I made up my mind that I had to be brave and take care of my sisters at all times because my mom was not fit. She used to scream at me all the time, "You're the oldest; take care of your sisters." Those words resonated with me like never before, and all awareness came forth that night. Also, funnily and ironically, I wanted to party at the Brass Key as an adult; go figure. My awareness as a child would pour into my attitude and mouth as a child, and I received a lot of whoopings for speaking like an adult. Whoppings, the ones that were well deserved, are not a part of my trauma, and I'm thankful for correction (we can agree to disagree here), but the abusive and uncalled-for ones are. It's abuse to whoop your child for things they do not truly understand. I used to get popped for saying I wanted my daddy, not understanding what my father was and what he had done to my mother. So many other examples, but I will just move on. I also remember my first trauma in school when I was in the first grade, and a child would pick on me every day calling me fat. This did not stop until I was in middle school and started fighting back, but one thing I do remember about the first grade is my late Uncle Alfred, ready to shut down the whole school and fight that kid. That was one of the first times I felt protected while dealing with what was mental trauma (small trauma and not that bad at that age, but enough to build and make me a fighter later in life). I continued down throughout my childhood being mentally abused along the way by other adults that really had no business around us. One of my mother's favorite cousins would literally feed her children and treat them differently when we were in her care. My mother's best friend's mother would antagonize and call me bougie and say anything spiteful towards my sisters and me whenever we were around. Again, small but significant and loud to me and my awareness. I know I was well aware because a lot of things my sisters don't even remember, and I'm actually glad they don't. Words can sometimes hurt a billion times more than anything physical. After so long, I grew numb to being whooped and did not despise them as much as I despised some of the people and the things they said that were let into our lives.

My childhood trauma did not just stop there; it actually reached its peak during my 10th-grade year of high school. I will never forget the morning my sister was having a difficult morning, and I asked her what was wrong with her! She started crying and told me that my mother's boyfriend at the time had been touching her and even peeking at her while she was naked through the peephole we had in our bathroom where a sock was kept vs a doorknob. I remember it like yesterday; my eyes are filled with tears for my sister to this day (not from a lack of healing, but from the compassion for a thirteen-year-old). I went and immediately told the person that was in charge of loving and protecting us, my mother. She quickly dismissed and accused us of lying, and I lost it. Everything in me was on fire; this was not our first rodeo with molestation. My same sister literally had just been molested two to three years prior. My sister was much different from my other sister and me; she was very skinny, timid, and quiet. She was also on Ritalin, because she was "hyperactive," and the medicine was so strong that she basically was a zombie anytime she took it. Me and my other sister were the polar opposite of that: loud, talkative, and spoke our minds at all times. I think because of my description of my sister, she was the perfect target for the predators that not only had been allowed in our lives but also authoritative figures in our lives. The first predator was a great uncle that lived in our family home, aka our grandmother's house. My whole family, at some point, lived in this home, and when my great grand-mother died, she left the house to him. My grandmother, of course, never moved, she had lived there her whole life, except when she was married. She grew up there, raised her children there, and took care of my great and great great grandparents there. We would spend the night there all the time; this was our second house because my mother was always out, and my grandmother kept us mostly. I remember us starting to have sleepovers, and my family never let us go over to other people's houses but ironically (you will understand the irony in a moment), people could come to ours. I remember when DHR came to my grand-mother's house and questioned our well-being and asked my mother and grandmother if they knew my uncle had been molesting my sister. I know you are wondering how they knew. My sister's classmate that spent the night saw what he did to my sister, and she went and told their teacher/school. They reported it to DHR, and then boom, every-thing was now out and exposed. They questioned my uncle, too, and he told them that he did not do it, but my mother knew he did. She knew it because she began crying and pulled all of us into a room and told us how he did it to her when they were kids and that the family only said he was trying to play "house." So, she and my grandmother both knew and believed my sister but wanted us to lie, so DHR did not take us away from them. I remember feeling numb in the beginning and bewildered, then later a lot more watchful of my sister and very protective; Lord only knows what my sister felt. We lied and stayed with my family, but God only knows that leaving may have prevented what we faced in the future. My sister had to endure unnecessary comments from my grandmother like, that probably would not have happened to you if you weren't always wearing short skirts and more berating things toward her. I know what I felt every time I heard something along those lines, anger, and helplessness! Anybody that knows me knows I love my granny more than anyone else in the world, but that was when resentment started to form for her (much later, we discussed this, she apologized, and we have since moved past this). She was a child; my sister was a child, one living in a single-parent household, so we were not conscious of proper clothing around males, also a very skinny child, so her shorts were not attention-grabbing, and again, a CHILD! It hurt; I will never physically, back then, know what it felt like to my sister, but trust me, it hurt me too. I told you guys at seven I knew I was our protector and that happening shattered all the protecting I thought I was doing. I just could not phantom what happened to my sister, my family. Outside of my mother, my family was my safe haven. I loved being around my grandmother, my great aunties, my cousins, and even my uncles. That last little bit of normalcy had been ripped away. The power I thought I possessed as a protector was ripped away from me, and my uncle, who protected me before in the 1st grade, had passed, and now my grandmother is not displaying the loving nature that was my comfort place. Now, fast forward back to the beginning of this story, my sister was molested again, and this time, my mom is vehemently denying the accusations. I guess now that it is her man, this time, it's different. Now we are liars, just want to be grown and don't want her to have a man in her words. I have no desire to see anyone in jail innocently, especially not a black man when I've been visiting my own father in prison since I was around five to seven years old. I know how sad and pitiful it is to go visit and be patted down, strip-searched, and then allowed to see your parent for just a small amount of time and cry from the time you see them, throughout the visit and all the way home. Imagine seeing someone that you love with all your heart be shackled and unshackled, told how close they can get to you, and be treated less than a human right in front of your eyes. That was a big part of my childhood trauma, visiting prisons, and to this day, my father is still there. There is no way I would subject another human being there or even their child simply because I do not like them. My mother is not only taking up for a man, but she is also now questioning our integrity and showing us that she loves him far more than us. I lost it and could not control my emotions anymore; I picked up a knife and stabbed his tires, busted out the windows in his car, and after fighting, arguing, and the police being called, I went to juvenile. I hated her, hated my life, hated this family. A few days later, we sat at a DHR hearing, and they told my mother straight in her face she had only two choices: remove him from home or lose custody of us. I guess she hated us too because she chose him, and we went off to different places. Imagine a person telling your mom she can have you if she just gives up the poison in her life, and instead of clinging to you, her child, she literally chooses a person that couldn't even be faithful to her. The amount of rage, hurt, and just desolation that was felt was enough for a lifetime and so much I would never want another person, especially a child, to ever feel in their life, and unbeknownst to me, this was just the beginning in our young life. I wanted to die, and I was fifteen. I should have been thinking about prom, dances, games, boyfriends, college, and any teenage things. Not this, but here we were, having to fight through life as kids and experience adult pain. According to the court, I was fifteen and old enough to go home with my grandmother, but since my uncle was already a pedophile on file, my sisters could not. My sister, right under me, was sent to a group home (dang near jail for teenagers, almost grooming for prison in my opinion and ironically like she was the person who had committed the crime) and my youngest sister to a temporary foster home. We're now split up, we have always been through things, but we were at least together during those times. Now, we're split up and visiting each other, and all we did was cry when we did. I could never have my heart broken again; this was it. My family had broken my heart before a man ever could; what is more hurtful than having your last free parent disown you and then the only other people that can honestly understand and feel you, that you exited the same womb from now also torn from you. My anger and emotions were boiling over, and it took my grandmother saying one smart thing to me about our mother for me to steal her car and run away. I was on the run for about two weeks, I had a friend at that time, and I stayed at her house some nights when her mother was not there, slept behind a church at night by myself, and was just surviving the best way I could. I cried and prayed so much and somehow thought of my mom's old friend that was so loving to us and called her. I really hate calling her now; you will understand why later, but remember I said this. I told her everything; she was so loving and concerned and agreed to try to get custody of all three of us so we could be together and begged me to take my grandmother's car back. Reluctantly, I did, packed, and left with her that day. I had nothing to say to my grandmother cause there she was, again enabling and aiding my mother. I felt justified in stealing the car because I was literally triggered over and over when she would try to spew negativity toward us in favor of my poor excuse of a mother. A mother's love has no end, and a lot of time in this world is the demise of many futures, progress, and diminishes accountability. My grandmother's love for my mother embodied that whole sentence.

2

Fostering Era (Childhood Trauma continued)

My mom's old friend was God-sent at that moment, even if we had to live with her, her four kids, and others. We were together, happy and safe. During this time, we were just getting back to normal, living with her and attending school and church. When we first went to stay with her, she was very into the church, nothing like what I used to remember about her. My old memory was her and my mother partying all the time, leaving us kids alone while they ran the streets. This current woman was filled with Christ, loving, and seemed to care for us. We went about our fostering life peacefully with her, except when my mother would come into the picture. She hated our foster mom/ fake auntie, and she did not want us near her, yes, the very woman that gave us up. She was always disruptive during her scheduled visitations, which I refused to go to. There were so many issues we probably went through twelve different social workers because they would give us someone new after every new event that happened. One of the major issues was that my foster mother still cared and had compassion for my mom, so she bent the rules after we stopped having supervised visitations. She would allow her to get my younger sister at times (my other sister and I did not want to go), take her places at times, allow her to call and talk, and do many other things, and that was the start of the chaos that soon pursued. When we first started living with our foster mother, I thought we had finally escaped the dysfunction we were accustomed to at home. Then the drama started; there were fights between my mother and foster mother because, as I said earlier, my foster mother was bending the rules. You know the old saying, give them an inch, they'll take a mile, and that is exactly what happened with my mom. When my foster mother did try to reel things back in, my mother started berating and harassing her to the point of a physical fight. All I can remember after the fight are the negative things said by my foster mother's mom and daughter. It was said that she should give us back to the system; we weren't worth the drama and anything we did, I mean even the smallest of things, her mom would say nasty things like that's why my mother didn't want us now. More mental abuse, more emotional abuse from people around my foster mother, and it was hurtful; imagine we dealing with this at home and still going to school every day. I'm in high school, and my sisters are in middle school. We were deemed bad; we fought, acted out in school and many other things, and were even talked about by church members. It was a lot of stress on our foster mother and us, so she finally moved into a new house with just us and her youngest son. Again, a short moment of peace, we all were in harmony and at peace, and slowly but surely, her older kids came to live, the daughter with two kids (her grandkids) and then her mother and now also a drunken uncle and frequent visits from her other friend and her four kids and just many more people. I got tired quickly and reluctantly went back to stay with my grandmother and continue going to school. I was also making a forty-five-minute commute from the east side of Birmingham to the west on the max bus to keep attending my Alma mater at the time. When I left, according to my sister, right up under me, even more hell broke loose. Outside of it being crowded, the home was basically teen ran, there were plenty of fights and inappropriate sex among some of the people in the household. There were also things going on like grooming, more abuse, and even murder. Yes, a murder, which we will get to in another chapter. This chaos led to my sisters eventually returning to live with my mother. Also, she swore to the courts and us that she had stopped talking to her boyfriend, the pedophile and that he had moved out for good. After my sister went back to live with her, my sister called me to come back to live with them so we could be together, and I did. I loved my sisters and was okay with my mother at this time since she was "done" with him. We were getting along fine, and then one day, he showed back up again, and just like millions of pitiful women, she accepted him back. Of course, we were not happy. For weeks he was still not staying with us, then boom, all of a sudden, he was living there again as well. I was so pissed off and disgusted with her that resentment started to set in all over again. I only continued to stay because of my sisters and because I had a boyfriend with whom I started to spend a lot of my time and was barely there. I was seventeen years old at the time and still a dependent of the state, so not in her custody, or anyone's for that matter. Also, staying with her versus with my grandmother, I had much more freedom. It was a weird and volatile living. The harmony that was there before he came was gone, and the house was filled with passive aggressiveness. One day, the stuff finally hit the fan, and an argument ensued between my mother and me that led me to tell her exactly how I felt about everything, including her man, and she put me out (choosing him all over again). At seventeen, I left her house and have never stayed with her again. I am now thirty-three years old. I was in an instant whirlwind because where was I going to stay? I called around, and one of my aunts told me to come and live with her. I did, but that did not last long at all. Although my aunt was a very loving, caring, and beautiful woman, she lived very differently from what I was accustomed to. I cried daily to my boyfriend about my living conditions, and one day, he said to me that he was going to get us somewhere to stay. He was nineteen, and I was seventeen, and three weeks after leaving my mother's house, we were living together in one of his father's properties. I was still a virgin, in high school, and now a full-time live-in partner. This was not ideal, and so many things could have gone bad here. This man could have beat me, raped me or forced me into sex, tried to take advantage of me financially or mentally, and so many things I've seen young girls go through. Thank God he was nothing of the sort! He was loving, caring, and a provider. I, to this day, praise his name for the way he treated and loved me. He is a great man, and I wish I had the same type of love to give to him that he gave to me, but I did try my hardest. We ran that household with peace and care, better than some couples in their thirties and forties. We were very in sync, and things were good between us. I continued on in school, and he worked; we were fine until my youngest sister came to stay with us and also until our place continuously got broken into. We stayed in the hood, and they robbed us blind on more than one occasion. The last time he said no, we're moving. My sister staying with me was only a problem because she was still acting out. Skipping school, hanging out with boys, etc. It got so bad that I was called to the office at my high school and told if I left school one more day, I would be suspended. Her school would literally call me because I had temporary custody of her and tell me to come to get her or talk to her. I would leave my school on one side of town and take the bus across town just to discipline or see about her. It got so bad that I could no longer keep her. She and my other sister eventually went back to stay with our old foster mother. We were all just living the best way we could, just surviving. My sisters both eventually dropped out of school and just did whatever. I finished high school and went to community college to pursue nursing. Before all this stuff happened, I planned to go off to college. I really should have, and you will see why in the next chapter, but my reality was different now. I was a homemaker with a wonderful boyfriend, had a full-time Manager job, and was trying to make something of myself. Me leaving now would not have made sense, and I needed and wanted to be near my sisters. We were somewhat distant but still in contact, and my need to be with them and protect them was so strong that it almost caused me to lose my own life and future.

3

Murder (You guessed it! More trauma)

I am now eighteen, a grown woman, and a responsible adult by law. I am at the start of the first semester of college, still working and living together with my boyfriend in a much better neighborhood. For the most part, life is stable and somewhat good. I'm grown, making my own decisions and putting in the work to have a brighter future. I am back in contact with some of my younger aunts and doing everything to just be happy. So, how by the end of this semester, I am facing attempted murder charges, and the bright future I just typed about is crumbling around me? During this time, my sisters were still living with my old foster mother and enduring a multitude of things. Some self-inflicted things and some not. I was always the person my sisters called on when things would get worse, and my foster mom and I would sometimes have words. It got so bad that we all ended up in a full-on brawl, including my boyfriend (who was a very passive and peaceful person). Even after that, my sisters stayed there. I kind of backed off from them, but only for a short amount of time. One day my sister right under me called me and told me that two of our foster brothers and their cousin had murdered someone. I was confused and just said, "Huh?" She said yes, they killed someone. She never told me who or went into more details about it, but she told me. I am not sure I believed her and kind of thought she must be tripping, and no way my foster brother/ play cousin was capable of that. He wasn't, but his cousin was, and that's who pulled the trigger. My foster brother was an accomplice, and another guy was an accomplice. This was just not anybody they had murdered; this was a young college-aged, innocent white girl from a very prominent family in Birmingham. They attempted to rob her while she was parked at a local school on the phone with a friend, sadly while following her family's instructions not to text or call while driving. When the cousin pointed the gun at her and tried to rob her, she freaked out and slammed on the gas, and he shot her; her car ran into a pole and stopped. He killed her for no reason, so young and dumb they did not even take anything, which was the motive. Not only did these idiots kill the girl, but they actually came home and bragged about it and told my sister every detail. She did not deserve that; her loving family did not either. She was not just a college student, she was a volunteer, worked the crisis hotlines, and was studying to be in psychology. My sister was shaken up; that's why she told me, but did not give me enough information for me to say anything. The girl's story ran on every news channel all day long for weeks. As I said, she was young, in college (my Alma mater, yea, some weird feelings were rising, while entering that building after the case), White/Italian, and her father was a prominent and wealthy bar and grill owner. She was making headlines, and every headline made my sister sicker and sicker. Then the fools that killed her cut one of her pictures out of the newspaper, placed it in a shoe box and labeled it their first kill. She, at that time, was the only one that knew they had killed her, and she was ready to confess. She never told me it was her that they killed; she eventually told my younger sister, and like a week after that, everything hit the fan. My sisters ended up fighting someone at the house for some reason, and they both ended up leaving my foster mother's house to once again live with my mother. During that time, I was still in touch with them but busy with my everyday life. I was happily enjoying my life, and one night, while my aunties were over and we were getting ready to go out, my sister called me and told me to come to get her from a party because it was drama. Yes, all four of us, me, my two aunties, and my boyfriend, went to go get her. Now before we went, I was already so pissed at my sister. She willingly went to this party, knowing that the very people she had been beefing with would be down there (our foster siblings and their cousins). When we pulled up to get her, she came outside and then would not get into the car. She kept talking about how her friend was inside and did not want to leave her. As we sat there trying to convince her to come on, her enemies started to emerge from the house, and we began arguing back and forth again. My sister still never got in the car. As we were arguing and on the verge of fighting, my boyfriend and aunties were screaming at me now to get in the car. The people at the party had started hitting my aunt's car with rocks, sticks, and trash cans. I finally got in, and we met my younger sister and her boyfriend around the corner at the store. I was livid at this point; I was steaming mad! Why would my sister not get in the car after begging us to come to get her? Why would her dumb friend not come out of the house? I was pissed off, and the fact that they were acting like they wanted to fight did not make it any better because one thing I could do and was good at was fighting. My sister's boyfriend was also pissed off because, at this point, we all had been screwed over at my foster mother's house and had fought someone for something, including him. He said come on, y'all, let's go back and fight. I was down immediately, was not even thinking straight, and was just overcome by anger. My aunties and boyfriend were not and tried to talk me into not going. They acknowledged that my sister should have brought her tail out and that she really was the one causing the issue to grow. They also stated that the people there all thought they were bad, but they weren't willing to return. I honestly should not have been willing to go back, and I respect all three of them for standing on that. I just could not let go of the fact they kept on disrespecting and trying us. My pride and ego were thinking for me at this point, and I said fine and got in the back seat of my youngest sister's boyfriend's car; my sister was in the passenger seat. We had planned to drive up to my foster mother's house and call them out to fight. When we got there, though, they were already outside. One of the girls, who really thought she was bad, picked up a huge rock and smashed it in the driver's side window. It caused the glass to go on him and my sister. My sister's boyfriend then lost it and pulled out a gun, which we did not know he had, and pulled the trigger. CLICK! My sister, me, and the girl all flinched, and time just stopped. Thank God the gun was still on safety! I mean, thank the Holy Trinity, Jehovah, Abba, Emmanuel, Jesus, the Holy Spirit, and every angel because we would have witnessed and been accomplices to now another murder. Once everyone else realized what had happened, the girl dropped the rock, and everyone took off running. Immediately after that, my sister's boyfriend took the gun off the safety and started shooting towards the house! I told my sister to get on the floorboard and stay down, and then he backed up and shot some more. He was so angry he would not stop. I told him to please pull off because the police would come. He finally listened and finally left. He was so angry he was crying (he also had just as much trauma as us) and still pointing the gun. I took it from him and said let's go home. I remember going to my aunt's house and downing a fifth of Wild Irish Rose. My nerves were so bad that it was my first time consuming alcohol.

4

Attempted Murder, Lessons Learned (Men, this may be your most relatable chapter)

Everything is spinning out of control now. We learned the next day that one of the bullets did not miss. One of my foster brothers was hit in the foot. The exact same one that was there during the murder of the girl. My sister, who had called me to pick her up initially, was so pissed off from the party and sad from the recurring headlines that she had already decided that she would talk about the murder, and she did. She told them everything, and my foster brother and his other two co-defendants were picked, along with the shoebox evidence and if I remember correctly the gun. I was still going to school and living like normal then, one day, a detective called. He told me that my sister had included me in her testimony and wanted me to come down to say my side of the story as well as tell them what happened the night of the shooting against my foster brother. I said cool and went in. When I got there, they initially asked me about my sister telling me about the murder, and I told them everything stated in the last chapter. Then they became more aggressive, asking about the shooting. Me and my sister's boyfriend both lied and said we were at a movie and were not involved. We decided to say it because there was no evidence to put us at the scene, and we felt if we stuck together on it, we would be good. Neither deviated from the story no matter how many times they asked us; they got so pissed and charged us both with attempted murder (My sister was still a minor, and they couldn't charge her, so they didn't). ATTEMPTED MURDER? For a bullet graze to the foot? This was definitely overkill, and I did not even pull the trigger. I went to the Birmingham city jail, transferred to the county jail, and stayed two weeks until I paid bail. I remember this all because it was near Christmas time, and I was supposed to be taking my final exams in all of my classes this week. I failed every single class of my freshman year in that first semester while sitting behind bars. I wasn't afraid of jail; I had been to Juvenile on more than one occasion while living with my mother, and I was bold and strong enough to fend for myself, but what I was afraid of was losing my whole future. I cried almost every day there on the phone with my boyfriend while he did everything to raise enough money for my bail. I cried for the fact that I was missing exams, the fact that now I have a pending felony, the fact that I am now incarcerated just like my father, and also the fact that while talking to the very sister that begged for me to come to get her, had the audacity to say to me she never told me to go down there. You know what, she was right in a way. She did call me to come to get her but never told me to get in the car with my sister's boyfriend, and while sitting there in my cell, I pondered on that. No, I would have never even been in the situation if she hadn't called me, but I still made a choice to get in that car to go looking for trouble. I simply came to fight, but one thing about looking for trouble you never know what measure of it you are going to receive. God dealt with me in that cell every day; He made sure before I left there that I understood completely what was happening and that I took accountability for my actions. I also knew that once I left, I would have to do the same for my sisters and stay out of their drama. I could no longer be their hero, and the cape was coming off. I felt like a failure; I felt defeated and like I was not going to survive this. God stayed with me during my time inside. A lot of times, I did not go into the general population. I barely ate and just listened to the other inmate's chats. They told me several times to snitch on my co defendant, and it crossed my mind, but there was no way I was going to do that. I have been accused of having too much loyalty, and I think I did with this situation, but also, even though I did not pull the trigger, I was just as eager to get over to that house that night, so I decided to woman up and see it through. After a long two weeks and almost beating up one of the inmates that was trying to pick with me because I wouldn't allow them to use my phone time, I was finally released on bail. I was overjoyed, not knowing what was to come, but for that moment, I was happy. Back in my loving Boyfriend's embrace in our apartment, who begged me never to leave him again and who had placed most of my bail money up, he and my aunt knew a lawyer, and some more friends and family had really come through for me. I was now back into freedom, but now this was a different type of freedom. Being free in America's society with a felony pending case or a record of any kind is not actually free at all. I learned this very quickly. After leaving jail and having the accountability moment, I decided that I needed to get back on track with what I was doing before that night, working and going to school. I went back for my second semester and had to take all my first semester classes over. My teachers were livid and told me that I should have had someone to tell them what was going on, and they would have saved my finals, etc. There was nothing they could do about it, and I accepted that and went ahead and re-enrolled. Work was a whole other situation; here is where America's jail system continues to work in oppression and constant re incarceration. I applied everywhere for a job. Every job I interviewed for, I would get, I mean, some jobs I was well overqualified for, but as soon as they pulled my background, I would immediately be told I was no longer considered a candidate. I had grown very independent and had been working since I was fourteen. I only did not work when I did not have transportation to work. To now tell me I could not work if I wanted to was a slap in the face. How are people with no income, let back into society on bail, supposed to survive without committing another crime? I mean, really think about it, no money, no job, and nothing to occupy our mind. It is a setup to keep people in the system (mass incarceration) because they usually turn back to crime to survive. Some people sell drugs, do robberies, sell their bodies, and many other things to make it in this capitalist society without work. I am not saying that companies should not be concerned, but I believe jobs should look at the individuals on a case-by-case basis and decide if they can hire that person. Since the pandemic a lot of these jobs, do not look at background checks or drug tests. It's okay when the companies are in need, but no grace is extended when the potential employee is in need. I was extremely smart, hard-working, and driven. I was never violent with people that were not trying to harm me and even worked for several years in a racist community without any incidents. I and many others like myself had made one mistake (not repeat offenders), and even though the slogan is innocent until proven guilty, we were already feeling the untold slogan which is really guilty until proven innocent. Not being able to provide for myself was very depressing for me; I hated it. I could not imagine being a man in this predicament, trying to take care of a family. I had a wonderful boyfriend who said don't worry about it, just go to school, but that was not enough for me. I had always provided for myself and kept in mind that he could leave me anytime. From a very young age, I was taught to never totally depend on a man, no matter how nice he is. Thankfully he never changed up on me, but I still wanted my own. It bothered me so bad I felt worthless, not good enough, and insecure about my current condition. I was able to now see through a different lens what a lot of people were facing every day in society. I then understood that being capable was not good enough.

I was so depressed about that and just about everything else going on that it started weighing on my relationship and my weight. All while going to school and trying to find a job; there was still so much drama going on in my life. My sisters were now deemed as snitches, and they were constantly fighting different family members from our foster brother and his cousin. It was always something every other day. The trial for the murder went on for three years, and my case depended on the outcome of that case. So many transitions took place during that time. My sisters both ended up pregnant during this time and, as I said, were being harassed and had to physically fight almost every other day with the family members of the accused. Of course, I was called every time. It was continuous drama and strife, my mother even moved to the other side of town, and still more things pursued. I had so much on my plate and was so stressed out that instead of gaining a freshman fifteen, I gained a freshman one hundred. This continued on until 2010 (2007 - 2010). After the final person was convicted, things sort of died down for a little while. My case was finally dismissed by the grace of God, and my Niece and Nephew were born.

5

A New Beginning?

If you are still reading, then you know that this young life of mine has been extremely chaotic, but now, fast forward to August 2011, I am at UAB in the Respiratory Therapy Program. It was such a triumph in my life because it took so much to get to this. I mean, you guys have read a lot of things I have been through, but let me break down my education track. As all the abuse, abandonment, and constant grief were going on in my teens, I was still attending high school. My foster mom lived on the other side of town from my high school, so I would get up at 5 a.m. to catch the first bus to the downtown station, then another bus to the other side of town just to get to class at 8 a.m. That was an ordeal in itself. I would fall asleep on the bus, they would break down, and homeless people and drug addicts would fight and curse each other, but I was determined to stay in school. I got into college at Lawson State, and as you guys read, I took all my 1st-semester classes over, and those classes weighted on my GPA heavily, my original major was Nursing, and your GPA mattered a lot to get into the program. I chose to switch to UAB through the STARS program to try to get into the nursing program there because I heard it was a lot easier to get in than at Lawson State. Once I got to UAB, my mentor looked over my grades and goals. He then told me directly to do Nursing there, I would need to take at least two more years of classes at UAB to qualify for the program because my GPA was lower at UAB. This was because of the added failed classes in the 1st semester (one mistake can have lifelong effects). He then suggested that I take a look at the Respiratory program because I would only need two more semesters of classes to achieve their GPA and prerequisite requirements. So that is what I did; I went to shadow at several different hospitals, and something just clicked. I really fell in love with the fact that we were still taking care of patients, but I did not have to be by the bedside of the same patients for the full shift, and respiratory was more specialized. Him sending me to shadow was a direct alignment of God's will in my life. I finished those semesters, applied, and got in. Once I got into the program, this was a new battle. A medical program at a top school of medicine is not lightweight. During those six semesters, I saw people crumble under pressure, quit under pressure, fail classes, and just not make it. We started with fifty students and graduated with thirty-two after a few students from the previous year were allowed back into the program. I worked and was a full-time employee at Walmart during this time. Every day, my teachers would tell me in order to be successful in the program, I would probably have to quit working. They did not quite understand what that meant for me because, unlike the majority of the students in the program, I did not have the financial means to actually not work. I was struggling. God did throw me a lifeline when one day, a customer I went out of the way to help asked me to fill out paperwork for a scholarship program through her church. I did, and they were very kind and generous to me. They paid my rent and gave me gas cards to get back and forward to school. They also later paid for me to take the prep classes for my boards and for me to take my boards. Along with paying off a portion of my student loans. I know that was a God send, I know this was all purposeful, and I loved them for everything they did and still do. Even though they did everything I spoke of, it still wasn't enough to meet my other daily needs. Water and light bills, clothes, toiletries, and food still had to be accounted for, but I was not going to ask them for anything else when they were already doing so much. So, I continued to work at Walmart until they fired me for attendance. I was going to work when scheduled, but not always on time. I informed Walmart from the time I entered the program that my schedule would have to change every semester and that I had no control over the days and times I had to go to class; this was no longer a prerequisite situation. I am now in a matriculating class and could not make my own schedule. They told me that it was fine, they would work with me, and quite literally did the opposite. So, in the third semester, I was unemployed. I then began seeking benefits from my unemployment and was the first person awarded the benefit from that particular Walmart, but it was only $86 a week. On one hand, being laid off was good. My grades in the program skyrocketed, and I quickly rose to the top of the class and became one of the most improved students probably ever in that program, per my professors. On the other hand, I now had to come up with the money for my utilities and everything else I listed earlier. I would sell my plasma at the plasma bank to get an extra $50- $75 a week. I did odd jobs, like passing out CDs for local rappers, I would do taste tests at local grocery stores through promotion companies to get money, and so many other things. I was determined; I went through so much and had to finish school. It was a huge goal of mine, and it was within reach. So, I could not stop, no matter the hurdle. I was halfway through one semester, and my car stopped working. Just completely gave out on me. I did not have any-one to call. My father is in prison, my mother is broke, and anything extra she did have was given to my sisters. The one time I asked my uncle for help in my early years of college; his wife quickly told me no. Outside of the scholarship, my grandmother was the only other person I had to call on, but even with her, she didn't have much or much to spare. My lights did get cut off one time, and she helped me get them back on. I simply made up my mind that I would walk to school every day even if I had to. It was well over two miles, but by this time, I had lost so much weight from working out to relieve stress and just trying to obtain better health that walking did not seem that bad. God stepped in again; two of my classmates (Heather and Cheyenne) overheard my car situation and decided they were going to help me. I dismissed them, of course, because I just was not used to being helped and did not want to come off as a person begging. They would not let up, and from then on, they let me ride with them to school and even would do extra stuff like tell me to go to the gym while they waited for me, etc. This was one of the kindest things that happened to me back then, and I'm forever grateful for them, especially since I did not fare well with quite a few of my classmates. I was totally different from them. Poor, outspoken, direct, misunderstood, and was loudly and proudly myself. You can only imagine the type of strife that brought along, while dealing with people from privilege, docile personalities, and over-the-mountain up-bringing. GOD had my back regardless of who did and didn't, and he made that very clear during that time. I even got called to my professor's office because of my background check. I knew they were going to put me out; I just knew it, but GOD! I'm in tears as I type because I know it was Him for them to tell me that they saw what was on my record, but still was going to allow me to finish my classes! I cried that entire day, so many things had gone on in my life and even in that program, but Grace was all on me! I finished the program after two years and passed my boards (two written tests and a simulation) on the first go around. Nothing but GOD and His divine will! After school, it took me three months to land a Respiratory Job, and I landed two! UAB and Princeton; I worked for them both and the fresh market for a while, just trying to get some type of financial stability. After a year and a half of being molded by the hospitals, I started traveling in my field (Traveling Registered Respiratory Therapist), going to different hospitals in different states, and working under high-paying contracts. I finally was making good money, not starving, not begging, not depending on anybody, and starting to live some of my dreams! I got a passport, started traveling internationally, exploring, and just living life! It really was a new beginning because prior to this, I had never tasted this level of satisfaction and fulfillment or financial well-being. All I knew was poverty, chaos, and hopelessness before. Now, I'm on cloud nine, dreaming again, living my best life, constantly in church ushering. Meeting new people, better people, and just pure happiness. Then in 2016, after working and traveling for three years in the states, I learned of an international travel position in Abu Dhabi, in the United Emirates of Arab. I applied for the job, and after sending loads and loads of paperwork, going through several clearances, and even taking an exam, I got the job! Wow, so now I'm going to live and work abroad! Life is just looking up; God is blessing me. I'm preparing from June 2016 to Jan 2017 to move my entire life to a new country. Like, what could be better than that? What could bring me down? I started celebrating with family and friends, having going-away parties, and spending time with people I love. In January 2017, two weeks before I'm set to board my plane to Abu Dhabi, I drove from Birmingham, AL, to Atlanta, GA, with a platonic male friend. We went out, and later that night, after partying, celebrating my new chapter that was about to begin, I woke up, and he was inside of me. Yes, HE RAPED ME!

6

RAPE

I woke up in the middle of him penetrating me and jumped up. I was so tired, drunk, and weak that I could only ask why he was on top of me and did he have on a condom; one of my biggest fears in life was being a mother. I just remember waking up and his hands on my breast; I pulled away and asked him why he was touching me. Then I jumped up out of the bed as I became more awake and aware and realized he had been intimate with me; I knew because I could feel it. I hadn't had sex in months at this time. I instantly started charging to the bathroom, and as I did, he grabbed my arm and said to me these very words, "I don't want you to think I took advantage of you." What else do you call it? What else do you call putting your penis inside a woman without her consent, permission, or acknowledgment? I was so distraught that I stopped thinking and went straight to the shower to get the hell out of there (anybody reading this, please NEVER SHOWER. If you can get away, go straight to a HOSPITAL, a RAPE KIT needs to be done, I have watched a million episodes of SVU, and this still never jumped out at me. Here it is now in bold letters, I NEVER WANT ANYBODY TO SUFFER THROUGH THIS). I dressed, grabbed my things, and went to my car. He followed behind me and kept apologizing, saying he was sorry. He was just upset about his dying grandmother. His Grandmother dying was not an excuse to RAPE ME!! I just looked, still in a daze, and said people wonder why I'm not very keen on men; this is why then I got in my car and began driving to Birmingham. It's Sunday; I was going to church as I had already planned. I cried the whole drive; everything in me was on fire, my insides, my brain, my heart, everything, and yet I was also numb at the same time. I had been hurt so many times in my life, too many. I must have been a fool to believe I was finally finding solace and happiness. Me? Laugh out loud, the girl who was born and bred in destruction from birth, the girl whose parents abandoned her, the girl who was always misunderstood, the girl who never fit in, the girl who fought most of her life had to be crazy to think that she was deserving of a better life than she had already lived. At least that is what I was feeling; that is what my mind was telling me. I went to church and cried throughout the entire service. It's a church, and so many people were crying that it was nothing shocking, so no one noticed my cries were actually for help and that I was dying on the inside. To be honest, whether it was at church or in real life, nobody ever knew when I was crying. I muffled so many cries in my life. Cry for what? Who is going to rescue me? I felt like God never saved me from one tragedy, yet He sent me to this terrible life I never asked for. I went home, I lived with my youngest Aunt at the time, and she came in with her bubbly personality asking how the trip was. I just said fine, closed my door, and went to sleep. I did not sleep the whole night; I woke up with the same nightmare. Every time I closed my eyes, I would wake up, and he was on top of me. Memories of the whole night kept coming back to me in flashes; I don't remember getting back to the room; I just remember him asking if I knew the directions and trying to keep me awake, and I couldn't stay awake. My next memory is me waking up a bit and him thrusting in me (This was when the rape occurred; many people have a hard time understanding what rape is. The moment he decided to stick his penis in me, without my knowledge, acceptance, consent, or awareness, it amounts to rape. Even if he stuck it in just once, it is rape. The rest of the details don't matter, but I have to be honest). I was so dazed I asked him if he had on a condom, thinking I was dreaming, then woke up a bit more, realized who it was, then jumped, and he moved off the top of me, and I grabbed my phone. I texted my aunt, who lived in Georgia and had met us at the club that night, and asked if she was home. He was towering over my back, and I did not respond, my back to him subconsciously; I knew he was watching me text her. I was so tired (I had worked out that morning, drove all the way to Atlanta, we went to dinner and had a drink there, and the club had several drinks there) and very drunk, I just said please stop, and fell right back to sleep. He did it again, and I couldn't even fight; my next memory was waking up the next day. When the sun rose that Monday morning, I was getting flooded with texts from him apologizing for what he had done. I was just cursing him out and telling him what he did to me. My aunt came into my room and asked me over and over again what happened and what was wrong, and then I told her. She was shocked and immediately pissed off and asked if I wanted to go to the police. The same police that are killing us? The same police I just dealt with during my trial? Police whom I have never seen protect or save? Also, I was too embarrassed to even talk to anybody about it, even her. I just wanted it all to be fake and go away. His cousin called me (my female "friend" at the time, whom I had met my rapist through) and asked me what had happened. Before I could even tell her what happened, she said out her mouth on speaker phone with my aunt next to me that she had talked to him and he told her everything, and she told him that was rape and that's why she did not trust men. I tried to just pray it away and keep going and live normally, but I was failing miserably. I went to work and stayed to myself. Some people quickly realized something was wrong because that was not how I behaved at work at all. Plus, it was my last two weeks; I should have been over the moon. I was not eating; I drank alcohol to sleep and still would wake up crying from the same nightmare over and over. It got so bad that I was not sleeping or eating. One night I tried to eat, I tried boiling an egg, took a few swigs of the crown, and went to shower. After the shower, I went right to sleep, only to be awakened by the fire alarm. My aunt and I ran downstairs; I had left the pot on the stove and almost burned down the entire condo. I was losing it horribly, and my aunt was not here for it and told me to call the police or she would. I just could not understand how I couldn't bounce back from this; after all, this wasn't my first rape and definitely not my first trauma. Trauma should have been my middle name by this time. Yes, you heard me correctly; this was not my first rape, but it was different. I'll explain why. My first rape happened on my mother's birthday one year. I met her after work and drank with her and her friends at the Handsome brute nightclub. After the club, I felt fine, so my coworker and I decided to go to a local strip club in town; I obviously was not fine because the club denied me entry. They felt I was too intoxicated. While waiting in line, I saw this dude I knew from Facebook. He was cool and tried to talk to me before, but I would not talk to him because he had a kid. Kids were a major turnoff for me back then, and as soon as a man told me he had a kid, I lost all interest. I was honest with him about that, and we decided to remain cool. We just talked over text from time to time. I didn't even really recognize him at the door, he made himself known, and I was like, oh hey, that's a friend. We had to leave because they were not going to let me in, so I went to the car with my co-worker. She asked me several times if I was okay, and I told her yes, I was okay and was going to drive home. I really did feel okay, and I had driven home irresponsibly drunk several times. I got in my car and drove home. I got home and remembered falling, going up my steps, and then finally making it to my door. I did see him, the guy from the strip club, and from then, everything was a blur. I remember him pushing my door in; that's it. The next morning, I woke up with vomit on the floor, hickeys, and a very sore vagina. At that time, I had been celibate for three years. I was dating, but no one was serious and was just focused on school. I definitely was not about to focus on someone whom I felt was not my type because of the potential baby momma drama. I had to sit there and realize what had happened. He texted me and asked him straight out why did he rape me. Do you want to know what his response was? Because he loved me, and because he thought I was beautiful and told me he was sorry. Y'all, how can a man I have never gone on a date with, never been in private contact with, never done anything, but speak over text and Facebook love me? I cried and cried and cried. I called and told my best friend what happened, and she came and just was with me, holding my hand, drying my tears, etc. I did not know what to do other than go get tested at the clinic. He kept begging and pleading with me not to go to the police because of his daughter. I blocked him and stayed with my friend. I prayed. Cried and just kept going. I was in the Respiratory Program, and I had no time to be sad, go through a case or do anything but pass my classes. I have no real recollection of what actually happened, so what could I tell? Other than that, he came to my house. My friend and I thought it over, we talked to her friend cop, and he said the text messages alone weren't good enough and that he was so sorry about what happened to me. I had never been that drunk before in my life. Me being drunk was still not an excuse for him to rape me. He knew I was unconscious and could not consent. Please, anyone reading, understand that no matter what this world tries to make you believe, it is not your fault. I didn't start drinking until I was twenty-one, by choice. I only started drinking after my ex and I broke up, and all the bad things in my life kept occurring. I also did not know my limits quite yet. I got over it; I think because I did not have the constant nightmares, the guy disappeared, and again I honestly had never met him in person in my life. With this new rape, this guy, I knew him. I trusted him. I thought we had developed a friendship, and he and everyone close to our situation knew I did not like him romantically, only platonic, and I had made that very clear several times. This was not my first time alone with him or sleeping in the same bed. Before this trip, he had come up to Birmingham from Mobile after Christmas to exchange gifts and to apologize again about New Orleans (See the next chapter). This trip to Atlanta was not even supposed to be a solo trip with just us. We were actually supposed to take this trip the week before, and his frat brothers, my aunt, his cousin, and my friend were supposed to come too. Me, him, my aunt, and his cousin were all going to share rooms. His cousin was like, I can get my own room, and I was like, why? You know me and him are not about to do anything, we are all friends. The week we all were supposed to go, this was for a fraternity thing they were supposed to have in Atlanta; it snowed. It snowed so bad between Birmingham and Atlanta that the fraternity thing was canceled (I really think God was trying to save me then, but I did not discern the situation, thinking it was just weather). He asked me to come to Atlanta with him the following week for his birthday. I said cool and wanted to get my hair cut by a barber there and see my aunt, who had informed me that she would not make it to my going away skating event. I invited my aunt and friend again that weekend, and both of them had to work. I worked out, drove to Atlanta, got my haircut, and met him in the room. We had made dinner reservations at Houston's, and he started crying as we were getting ready. He told me his grandmother was dying. I gave him words of support and told him we did not have to go out if he did not want to. He said no, let's go because he did not want to sit and think about it all night. We went to Houston's as planned and had dinner. During dinner, he asked me why I changed the engraving on the watch I had got him for Christmas during the exchange (How did he even know I had changed it? The cousin. I was really dealing with a group of people that were not trustworthy, lacked discretion, and had several conversations behind my back). I told him straight up that I had changed the end of it because I originally had "Love," Krys on its end. I told him I changed it because I did not want to confuse our relationship as more than anything other than friendship. He told me he understood and that it's smart to communicate clearly (The Irony!) We then left the restaurant and headed to this local club in town called Josephine lounge. We started drinking when we got in. He told me he had gotten sad about his grandmother again. I asked if he wanted to go, and he said no, that he just wanted to have a good time. Then my aunt showed up, and we kind of split up. I was walking around the club with my aunt, drinking and celebrating my leaving! I'm about to move across the country one hour outside of Dubai! I'm too lit at this time. People were buying us drinks left and right. I met this super fine African guy, and he invited my aunt and me to sit in his section. He was cool; we exchanged numbers and hung out the rest of the night. The platonic friend came around only to give us drinks, and I did not see him anymore until it was time to go. I remember getting in the car and him trying to get me to hold the GPS and put the address in, but I couldn't. I was already drifting to sleep and was too drunk to function. I told him that and also told him when I got to the room, I was going to pee and go straight to sleep. The next memory is me waking up with him inside of me. He would have never tried that if I was sober, and he would have died with me fighting him off of me if I was coherent enough to do so. Now, fast forward, I did call the police. Birmingham police are furious and want to pick him up, but tell me that since it did not happen there, I had to call Atlanta. I did that and had to drive to Atlanta to file a formal police report. I did, and it's at the Fulton County Police department. I gave them all the text messages, told them everything that happened, and identified him and everything. The detective told me that he had to talk to the accused as well and then move forward. The assault counselor came to speak with me and told me they would do everything in their power to help me and that even if I did not get justice, they would always have a record of it (Remember this conversation). I left with a bit of hope and went home. The detective called me again a few days later and asked when I would be leaving the country. I told him I was set to leave on Jan 31, 2017. He told me OK; he was going to try to have something set up before then. He didn't and actually did not get back to me with a date until I left the country. I will discuss this more in the second part of the book.

7

Betrayal

Again, everyone close to this situation know he raped me. I never gave him an inkling that I liked him romantically after seeing him fully (his actions/ how he moved). The cousin knew that my so-called friend who was involved, and even his frat brother knew. Let me give y'all some context to understand. I met the female cousin through another friend out of town at a birthday celebration one July. We had a lot of fun, spoke a lot during the celebration, and talked about travel. She told me how she desired to travel but did not have the appropriate people to travel with. I gave her my number, and we kept in contact and developed a relationship. The following February, we traveled to Canada together for an all-star game weekend, and it was good; she got along with my crew, so she was now like family. Her cousin tried to talk to me then, via her, but I was in a relationship and loyal. Then we started planning a trip to Barbados that Summer and the male and his friends were supposed to join and didn't, through the entire trip, he constantly asked about me. She asked if he could have my number, and I told her yes; this was like August, and I had been single since March. We talked. He was not really interesting, but he was nice, so I let it roll. I'm single and dating, so we'll just see what happens. He came to Birmingham from Mobile in October for Magic City Classic and asked if he could see me. I said cool, we hung out one night, and that was it. I did see him at the Classic game, and his friend and a friend of mine exchanged numbers. Then in the first part of November, the female cousin got a new place, and he and I were still talking. So, my friend and I drove to Mobile to celebrate the female cousin's new place and ended up surprising the boys after. My friend and I left with the boys and went and had drinks and did karaoke. My friend went with his friend, and they slept together on their first meet-up. He tried to take me home, and I told him no, that he should take me to his cousin's house, and he did. The next day we were all talking, and a couple of things came up. One was that the friend had told my friend that his friend did not know how to "handle" me. Whatever that means, and two, we all sat and talked about relationships at waffle house. My friend was talking about how she felt things quickly and was head over heels over the friend (whom she had just had her first face-to-face with). I told everyone at the table, including him, I don't operate like that, and it takes me time to get to know someone. We had just met face to face in October; at this point, it is still the beginning of November. That was example number one. In the second example, I took the test and passed it for the Hospital in Abu Dhabi, and we talked regularly, so I told him about it. He then asked me to go to New Orleans with him to celebrate and attend a basketball game. My friend and his friend were coming as well, so I said sure. He joked on the phone about getting two beds and me wearing a chastity belt. I told him if he would keep his hands off me we didn't have to get two rooms. We went to the game and then met up with the friends on Bourbon Street. His frat brother didn't plan anything for them two and really only wanted to lay up. That was none of my business because if you don't demand respect, you won't get it. We had a ball on Bourbon, got drunk like everyone else there, and I danced the night away with everyone in the club and even our cab driver. I love to dance (Remember the dancing part, y'all). We got back to the room, and he tried to give me oral which I did not oblige, and reprimanded him about it the next day at breakfast in front of everyone. He said he wouldn't try that again, and that was that. We went to dinner the next day, and at dinner, we started talking, and he started saying very eye-opening things that were a major turn-off for me. During the conversation, one of the things he said to me was that his frat brother had asked him why he was doing so much for a girl he had not slept with. He kept talking about all these things other men were saying, and I grew more turned off by the minute. Why was this thirty-something, almost forty-year-old man discussing what we talked about in private? Why was his friend so worried about me? This was his friend's second time making remarks about me when I never said anything about him or to him. Why were he, my friend, and his friend on three ways discussing me? I asked him if he told his friend I never asked to go anywhere or for anything he was giving to me. I had been to three international countries by this time, and New Orleans was just a six-hour drive or two-hour flight from my hometown, which I had visited before. I don't know why he or his friends thought that I would be impressed by an out-of-town trip two states over or that this was a lot of money. Many men had taken me out of town, several I had not slept with, and it was never a requirement or contingency to do so. I was completely grossed out at his lack of backbone and directness. If he wanted to sleep with me, all he had to do was ask, and I would have politely said yes or no. I was no virgin but had been celibate for years on and off. If I wanted to do something, I would do it and did not need to be coerced into it. After I started questioning him, he got quiet, and that ended the dinner. The next day I left without saying another word to him after dinner. I then went home and blocked him. His cousin begged and begged me to unblock him for weeks (later on, when stuff really hit the fan, she said I should have never unblocked him, even though she was begging me to... yea). He kept telling me he was sorry and that he would never publicly discuss anything between us again. I should have blocked them all, because she was just as insistent as him. I finally answered and told him straight up we could never be because I do not roll like that. As transparent as I am, I did have discretion when it came to certain parts of my life. A grown man discussing what we were doing was never it. We were never going to grow organically with this many people involved in our situation, and at that point, I was completely uninterested in anything. He asked me to please at least allow him to be my friend and begged me to come around Christmas to exchange gifts as we had planned prior to the fallout. I reluctantly obliged because up until the trip, he was nothing but a gentleman to me and was very apologetic. He came a few days after Christmas and hung out with my aunt and me; we went to grab drinks and just talked. He was telling me about all the hardships in his life, like his family relying heavily on him for financial things, paying for his niece's daycare, feeling like he had no one, and that everyone in his life was just using him. I'm an empath, so not only did I understand through my own experiences from everything he stated, I felt for him and sympathized with him. After the bar, I felt like I was ok to be his friend and told him that. He told me that I was going to make a man very happy in marriage one day, so I assumed he understood, we were friends, and nothing further would come of that. He spent the night at my aunt's house with me and did not try anything, and was cool. The next time I saw him was in Atlanta when he raped me. You know, the craziest thing about the rape is, not only was I raped but I was also blamed for my rape and had two friends, women friends, close to the situation new details and dang near aided him in his attack on me. Let me tell you why I say this. After the rape, I told y'all his cousin admitted to me on speaker phone with my aunt that he told her every detail, and she stated it was rape. She was texting me regularly, telling me how she admired my strength. How she hated what happened to me, and even her mother was writing to me on Facebook asking me if I was okay and everything. Then she stopped; I eventually blocked her because seeing her still go along like nothing happened was too much to bear. We did have a conversation after this when I mailed a letter I had to write in counseling to my rapist (I'll explain this later in detail). She then said to me that I should have never unblocked him, and I said girl, you begged me to, daily. She also told me she would never stay in a room with a man she did not intend to sleep with, and I told her, unlike her, I wasn't free with my vagina. I had stayed with so many men and never had them do anything inappropriate, especially not the men I considered friends. A rapist is a rapist, not all men are rapists, and if I were to walk around with that mentality, I would literally be terrified of men (I am, to an extent) and labeled bitter or crazy. I also had men do things for me for many years for nothing in return. I wasn't trying to play them or get over on them or anything, we were just cool, or they thought I was beautiful. Some men sowed seeds into my future because they felt as if I could make it and respected me for being in college grinding for my degree. If a woman lying beside you or near you is sleeping or is drunk or both, and you decide to put your penis inside of her without her consent, you are a rapist. If this is not your wife, girlfriend, or a woman you had ever had any sexual contact with. Also, she had to be saying things about me. Why did he know about the engraving? Why would she tell him about the engraving at all? I then understood that she was not a friend and probably only contacted me initially for information. If not, then what other purpose? Her whole attitude had changed, and she never told the story he told her that she stated was rape. I had only known her for maybe a year and a few months before the rape. My friend, the friend that went on the trip, the one that was dating his friend, etc., went way back. I had known her for eight years. We met while working at McDonald's together, and I had shielded her from being bullied, and we became friends from there. We had been through so much together; I even saw her have her first child. Why would she tell me after she finally found out about the rape, (It took me a minute to verbalize to anybody, even my aunt I stayed with. Rape is a process, just like grief. Yes, sometimes it takes time for women to speak on it.) that the guy had told her and his friend in the room in New Orleans that he thought I was going to let him have sex with me, by the way, I was dancing. Again, this was way after the rape. So, essentially, this man had been plotting on me for a while. She was so caught up in trying to be with his friend that she failed to mention this to me at all. She even tried to tell me to cheer up. It was okay because she had been molested. Being molested and raped are two different things (both very traumatizing), and I feel like she only said that to try to get me not to press charges. Then after that, she went on a slander campaign against me. She literally called my sisters to try to tell them about things she thought they did not know about me or would judge me by and also tried to make it seem as if somehow I deserved the rape. Before I go any further, let me say this, no one deserves to be raped. Even if maybe you did have too many drinks, even if you decide to go somewhere alone with someone, even if you do dress trendy or provocatively, even if you dance all night long, even if you say yes at first, then change your mind, even if you were to walk down the street naked, not even then. No one deserves to be raped. Women that wear hijabs and shaylas or nuns, fully dressed women from head to toe, are raped. People are raped because the person is a rapist, and that is that. Whether it was a misjudgment call on their part, or even if he is sorry or says he is, he still has raped someone. This girl went on to try to tell my sisters about past endeavors of mine that weren't secrets and then tried to berate my dancing habits as if my dancing was a crime. Both my sisters, to this day, want to strangle her and definitely did not understand her point, nor did they believe her. I told them all the true parts, and they again asked what that had to do with anything, which did not excuse my rape. This girl, to this day, sees my friends and loved ones and harasses them with questions about me, and talks about how she misses our friendship. Apparently, she and I have two different meanings for friendship. People will never cease to amaze me on planet Earth.

Part II Now Let's Heal...

In order to heal, you have to first recognize you need it. In this part of the book, I will walk you through what led me to seek the help I needed and deserved. I will also walk you through everything I had to go through after recognizing it. Healing is a journey, and it is not passive. You actually have to work, fight and advocate for it. It is not easy most of the time; you will become tired, and over the journey, you will still have triggers from time to time, and you will still be wondering why certain things ever happened. Once you get to the point I am at in my healing; things finally take a turn for the better. Life becomes more beautiful, questions that bother you come with answers, and you change and grow. Healing is a process worth going through, and the reward is GREAT and much better than the alternative of being un-healed. being unhealed is damaging, keeps you in a certain place, and is nonproductive. I also will touch on this during this part of the book.

8

The Continued Build UP

On January 31, 2017, I landed in a brand-new country, a new world, Abu Dhabi, United Arab Emirates. I am overjoyed and yet very sad. I was not supposed to be like that. I am supposed to be proud of myself and happy about my future, but honestly, every second of every day, I can only think about dying or killing my rapist. I did everything as normal, only because I woke up again but prayed daily never to wake up again. On February 5, 2017, I started my new job; I got up, dressed, combed my hair, and went to my new job. I put on a brave and happy face and even met one of my good friends, whom I am still close to this day. We're in orientation for weeks, and I got up and went every day, enjoyed the people I was around, and actually built a bond with my orientation group. Every morning I would go and give them that charming, beautiful glow and smile, and every night, I would go home and cry myself to sleep, hoping I didn't wake up. At this point, I am a walking, living paradox. The people around me did not know what I was facing or even recognize what I was dealing with. They only saw the brighter side of me, and I never truly revealed what was going on within me (Most will just be reading it in this book). Also, during this time, I was in constant contact with the detective over my case. They set my court date to March versus before I left the country. He told me no matter what, if I let him know when I was coming home, he would give me a scheduled court date for when I was home. I already knew I was coming home in July because a formal friend of mine was getting married, and I was a bridesmaid. I told him when and he sent me over the documents with the directions on how to get a new court date. So, for six months, I suffered in silence and portrayed normalcy while dying. I knew this wasn't healthy, but I continued on. What was I really supposed to do? Now also in a foreign country. Every time I opened my mouth to pray, nothing came out. I was so angry with God; how could He allow this to happen to me? I had already been through what seemed like three billion things, and now this. I also was being what I considered obedient before the rape. I was at church almost all week; I went to bible study on Tuesdays at my church, Wednesdays to my aunt church, and then Sundays back at my church; I even was an usher at my own church. I paid my tithes, read the bible, and prayed constantly, so what did I do to deserve this? I could not wrap my mind around it, so I just stopped talking to Him, and He also stopped talking to me. Even when I did listen to a sermon, it never penetrated me. To have God or hear Him, your heart and mind must be open and receptive; I was neither. I sought counseling through our hospital counseling program, which helped me not to go completely insane. The therapist was a very kind and quiet woman from Romaine or Israel, I can't remember, but she was extremely nice, caring, and helpful. She always listened, never judged me, and always assured me the things in my life were not my fault. I was kind of having a hard time believing that because at this point, it was somebody's fault, God's, my parents, my ancestors!? I couldn't prove exactly who, but I was over it. She helped me get to a decent space, and then I went home to visit. As the detective stated, I went to the courthouse on my last day to fly back to Abu Dhabi, and that was a mess. I was given the run around at the courthouse and quickly came to find out the detective had given me the wrong address and directions, "mistakenly." I cried that whole trip to the airport and took several pills to stop my head from hurting and possibly O.D. One of my closest friends, Cheyenne, was on that flight with me and told me she watched my breathing most of the trip. She even bought me my favorite candy and dried my tears. I went back to Abu Dhabi, and the cycle of being mad, hurt, and wanting to die started all over. I did go back to counseling, but only briefly. My job decided that they were going to cut the funding and start in-house counseling, and I was not sure how and when, so I suffered in silence. I did talk to my friends that I knew and my aunt a lot, but it really did not mean much because I felt like I was wasting my time. There was nothing they could do to help me unless you've been raped. To me, you could never understand the magnitude of feelings, hurt, and pain that come along with it. Some people reduce it down to just sex but trust me; it's so much deeper. It's almost like getting robbed; you know that feeling of did this just happen, then the level of innocence and peace get taken from you, and now you are just bewildered and unnerved. You don't want to even live in the home you loved so much before the robbery anymore. Like that, but fifty times worse. I was now paranoid and aggressive towards innocent men. I had never been sweet on them anyway because prior to the rapes, a host of other men had already destroyed what a natural encounter with the opposite sex should be like. My father abandoned us in prison; my uncle molested my sister, and my mother's man did the same; then the men that were supposed to be in my life for greater reasons (mentors) reduced our relationship down to a sexual advances. One example is, a pastor, married man, and domestic violence coach whose class I was attending told me to come and pick up my certificate from his office since I missed the graduation day for an academic class.

I went, and before he gave me the certificate, he sat and told me how beautiful I was and every nasty desire he had for me. I was so shocked I only uttered no thank you, took my certificate, and left. I called my boyfriend at the time and cried and told him what had happened. Then there was this other time I went to see my family's lawyer, another married man I looked up to. He was always supportive and gave me and my boyfriend sound wisdom on relationships, life, etc. I don't know what happened, but that day I was in his office with him alone, and we talked about life as we usually did. When I got up to leave after our conversation, which included me asking about his wife and daughters and him asking about my now then ex-boyfriend, he gripped my butt and told me I was beautiful and that he would take care of me. I just looked at him, then left. I was so hurt; I called my ex-boyfriend again, cried, and even threw up a little. I started to hate my beauty at this moment, like I should not have to make myself smaller or dim, to not be preyed on by men who were supposed to be positive representatives in my life. My ex-boyfriend, my first, was really the only man in my life that I had to hold on to and say all men aren't like that. Then my best guy friend Kendall was so kind, loving, and giving to me and never tried to do anything sexual to me, we also had been to several places, drank together, fell asleep together, shared rooms, etc. many times, and he never did anything to me. So, for years, I tried to overcome the horrible things I had experienced with men, then years of toxic relationships, and now two rapes. I was done. Any man that slightly offended me felt my wrath. Not that they did not deserve any of it, but maybe not to the extent they received. Not just men, any and everybody, but especially men. I was walking, talking blaze of fire. October 2017 came around, and I went home again. It was my grandmother's 70th birthday, and I helped plan, put together, and get her to her surprise birthday party. That was joyful; I always felt joy when helping or doing things for others, just not for myself. After all of this, I went to Atlanta on my last day in the U.S., and again at the courthouse, I got the runaround. The clerks and even the Atlanta Magistrate tried to help and couldn't, but one thing they did discover was that I was again at the wrong courthouse. I was given the directions and full address by this same detective. He told me that was the correct courthouse and that I needed to follow the directions. I had not another minute to spare, or I would miss my flight. I got on the flight hoping, wishing it crashed and not that everyone died, only me. I have every email, and court document for everything I have mentioned in this book, and some things, like the murder trial, can actually be googled. I say this because I know at this point, you guys are reading this and probably saying this stuff cannot be true, and I assure you it is, and I have very uncomfortably lived through every detail.

Months go by in Abu Dhabi, and I'm still suffering but living at the same time. It was a popular meme during this time that said, somehow I am living my best and worst life at the same time and it truly resonated with me. On socials, you could see me traveling the world, going to brunches and many different exhibits, etc. I did everything, but I had always been very outgoing. Plus, doing things, especially traveling allowed me to escape my horrid existence. I visited like ten plus countries during my 1st two years in Abu Dhabi. While still suffering the side effects of being unhealed. I was also very triggered all the time. During this time, R. Kelly and Bill Cosby were both finally being exposed and put on trial for their sexual crimes against women. Those women were being berated and accused of lying as if this type of stuff did not happen often and daily, regardless if the man was rich, poor, black, or white. The #Metoo movement had happened, and again, every victim that spoke out was slammed or picked apart by people who actually think women are just running around lying. I do not know what it will take for this country to see women as victims, especially sexual victims, especially Black women. No matter what happened, somehow it was the woman fault or some type of conspiracy to bring the black man down. This is not an I hate men or black men speech; it's pure reality and can be seen every day, especially in social media commentaries, etcetera. Then even when I did log out of socials and stopped news emails from coming to my phone, I still was in an atmosphere of black women being berated at work. I worked closely with a black man who had something negative or condescending to say at every turn towards black women in my department. He would then go out and date the non black women at our job; that were culturally appropriating black women. I did not care about this too much because I do not care about interracial dating; it was the constant comparisons to black women that made no sense. This was a daily thing; he was so angry that a black woman was being promoted over him that he even went and lied on her saying she was showing favoritism and more things that were baseless and found to be untrue. Then there was a Mexican man that constantly spoke ill of Black people in general that I almost came to blows with. Those were the things in UAE; even more, drama and confusion were going on back home. In the USA, my grandmother had a stroke; my sister had murdered her boyfriend in self defense, people that I knew were dying, etc. There were so many things going on constantly triggering me, along with what I had already been going through, that one day I burst into the employee health office and demanded a counseling session or told them I might hurt someone. They gave me one measly session with my old therapist. I started turning to other things I had never done before. Women, weed, more alcohol, sex without any emotional connection, and if my partner acted emotionally, I would ghost them and probably more things I have yet even to discover. I was a mess, alive, not living, not thriving, not growing, not transitioning, just breathing, going, and surviving.

9

The Wake-up call

In December 2018, I went home for Christmas. On this visit, instead of waiting until the end of my trip like I usually did to go handle my case, I planned to handle it as soon as I got off the plane. My mom and aunt came to get me from the airport, and we went right to the courthouse. When we showed up at Atlanta magistrate office, we talked to multiple people and one of the detectives and looked over all of the email evidence, and they told us that the directions the Detective gave me were wrong. He told me he was so sorry I had to go through this and that he wished it was in his jurisdiction because he would have had my rapist arrested, not talked to, and would have made sure I had my day in court. He told me not to call or email that detective anymore; he told me instead to go straight to the police department and talk to another detective. By the time we left there, it was dark, and all the offices were closed, so we got a room and stayed overnight in Atlanta. The next day, we got up and went to do exactly what he told us to do. When we got there, they tried to shut us down and make excuses for the detective over my case. Then, they finally found my file and tried to talk to me. One officer even had the audacity to say to me, "oh, we were trying to make sure everything was true before we did anything, and I said to him bluntly and boldly that I woke up with a man (expletive) inside of me that I did not ask or agree to being. His whole pale face went red, and then he found the paperwork to tell me what courthouse to go to. We went to this small courthouse in Fulton County. This was not at all the address or courthouse the original detective told us to go to. He had been sending me to the downtown Atlanta headquarters when this happened, I was interviewed, and everything else pertaining to this case was in Fulton County. Two totally different areas, jurisdictions, and courthouses. Yes, for almost a year, I was getting the runaround; yes, me the victim. We get to the courthouse, and the same things are happening; they were all running around saying that they could not refile because nothing was ever filed. I showed them the original court document and emails etc. They had not even heard of my rapist's name; that right there, I think, was the most triggering. My mind went all the way back to my first interview with the detective and abuse advocate. She assured me that no matter what happened, my case would always be in the system, even if I did not go further with the prosecution. I cared more about that because there could be another victim or attempted victim. What I was suffering through, I never wanted another woman to experience in her life. These people had really spat in my face, and I just wanted to leave; they were not trying to help us. One sheriff was running all over the building trying to get different people to look into it and see what they could; he really tried. He was just as pissed and looked like he wanted to cry as I was. It was really nothing else for him to do. I just told them to let's leave, my mother and Aunt. I was so pissed off at myself. Why did I not kill this man with my own two hands versus telling anyone what happened? Why did I put any type of trust in America's very flawed, racist, and sexist judicial system? Had I not learned anything from my father's railroaded case? I was so emotionally spent that I decided that day to give up and recognized that I had to leave it alone in order to move on. People always ask why victims don't speak up or wait for other people to come out; well, as you can see in my case, look what they go through. To be believed, men dang near got to rape at least three women or rape them on camera. Saddest of it all, I had a witness that my rapist told every detail that could testify to him admitting he did it, but it's his cousin, my ex-friend. I had to let that hope of justice sail. That was one of the first things I recognized and started seeking help on how to heal. At this point, nobody was talking about healing other than church and a few people who had actually gone to therapy. Most churches only talked about it vaguely, with no real steps or ways to go about it. They talked about healing the medically sick and healing people from demonic ways, but never the mentally sick, the trauma sick, the emotionally sick. My pastor would always say, healing is active, not passive, which I do agree with, but what does that mean? The meanings he gave were factual but lacked impact on me. He could have been preaching better than I was receiving, but it did not penetrate me at that moment. The best series he's ever given on healing is the series we're in now, OUCH 2022, The Rock City Church, Birmingham, AL. I had to do deeper work and started researching and seeking the meaning of healing and how to heal. I literally went home after my vacation to Alabama, so heavy and burdened. It was now 2019, and I had just come back from Abu Dhabi. I went to Alabama the beginning of December, at that point still fighting for my case, and by the end of the month, my grandmother had a stroke. Something had to shake because I literally, by this point, was the walking dead. I am dead on the inside; on the outside, no one really knew. I was still so disoriented that I blurted out my rape in a group I thought was a safe place, and it was not, but a person in the group reached out to me separately and told me she had faced the same fate not too long ago with sexual assault. We started learning and talking to each other, and now I had an ally, someone who could fully understand my plight. I had friends and family that were very empathetic, loving, and supportive during this time, but they couldn't understand because they had not been raped. The friend talked a lot about healing, her healing journey, and forgiveness. She was in a much better space than me at this point mentally and her talking to me and sharing with me was therapeutic and a bit of the help I needed. I started searching for books on amazon to read and help, and there were none that resonated with me and quite few (one of the reasons I am writing this book). I was pushing along but still not quite understanding or recognizing my healing journey. I was still barely speaking to God, and as you can hear from the reckless things I was doing, despite all, He still had His hands on me. The fact that he still had His hand on me started constantly being a thought, but it was always silenced by the fact that I still felt as if He allowed all my traumas to happen to me or that He was willing to forgive rapists. He promised salvation and forgiveness to all who came to Him, which was just not sitting right with me. Then I heard a sermon or read somewhere that God would never elicit pain in us, but He would use our pain for greatness. This was said and backed up by several scriptures that I read for myself and understood that His only goal is to prosper us (Romans 8:28, Jeremiah 29:11, John 2:16). I grew up hearing all my life that what the enemy meant for evil, God changed for good. I didn't even know it was a real Bible verse (Genesis 50:20), I just thought it was a saying, but after understanding what had happened to me and who was behind it, I truly knew there was no way God would cause those traumatic things that had occurred in my life. The Bible literally tells us that we will have trials and tribulations (John 16:33), evil lurkers that are seeking to devour us (1 Peter 5:8), and even let us know that we are at war, not against flesh and blood, but principalities and powers (Ephesians 6:12). This all seems mysterious and unreal until you really go through and understand we're truly living everything the Bible has already told us in reality. I then started thinking to myself, if I am going to be alive, I need to live to my fullest; He wouldn't let me die like I had been begging to, so I re-enrolled in college. I was going to finish my prerequisites for the PA Program and then apply. As I was doing that, my aunt was telling me her friend was in the PA Program and how she would love for us to talk. So, she gave me her number, and we talked about PA, and she was very nice and down to earth. She literally told me how it was nothing but God that she got in the program, and I was just Amening her, and then out of the blue, she said, how are you with God? That was such a peculiar question for me at the time. I did not know her, and I knew my aunt was not discussing me with her. That question was the question that needed to be asked; I told her honestly, "Not in the place it should be." She told me that that was okay, but it was time. I heard her; rather, I heard Him. After talking to her that day, I hung and began to cry and pray, cry and pray; for the first time in two years, my tongues came out. I had not prayed that deeply or sincerely in two years! Two years is a very long time not to have God in your life! If something happened to me in those two years, I honestly can't tell you where I would have gone in the afterlife. God was sending a raft out to me to save me from further destruction and pain. I was so blinded by trauma, pain, and hurt that I felt like He had stopped talking to me when in all actuality, I couldn't hear from Him, and I was the one that stopped talking to Him. To hear from God, you have to have an open heart and listening ear or what the Bible calls a contrite spirit (2 Corinthians 7:10). I was down and out, tired, so by this point, that's all that I had.

10

Move to Action

After that prayer and my tongues came back, I started praying again more often. It was slow because everything else in me was still fighting to hear and love God the way I did before. I can't remember quite when, but I remember my church starting something called Devo energy. It is a daily devotional on YouTube that includes my pastor and other church members on a panel to pray every morning and then eventually dissect and analyze whatever scriptures or sermons my pastor had preached. I did not miss a Devo; through these, my faith in God was being restored, and I was gaining momentum back for Him, His word, and His love. It was also around this time I started looking at myself in the mirror. I mean, really looking at myself, not my outer shell but everything about me. My time in Abu Dhabi was coming to an end. I had seen and done enough. I opened my eyes to how being there was adding to my cycle and trap. I remember talking to one of my friends on the phone one day, and I was complaining about my job (I hated my job in Abu Dhabi, not the work or pay, but everything else). She flat out said to me, I've known you a very long time, and I know all the terrible things you have been through, and I have never heard you complain this much. That was a big eye opener for me and was the nail in the coffin to let me know I needed to make some decisions in my life and decided that would be my final year in the UAE. I had been complaining about that job for about two years straight, I told y'all earlier some of the things that went on in the department, but many other things with the patient care irked me as well. I came from a level one trauma center, and the way we cared for and treated our patients was light years ahead of this facility. Also, the healthcare workers were not protected or really allowed to practice as they normally would. I saw family members berate, threaten, and almost come to blows with several of the employees while just trying to do their jobs. In America, they would literally ban people from the hospitals or arrest them, but not in the UAE; the families were always right. That was just one of the many things that I was tired of. Also, I had begun to be over the social scene in the UAE. I had been to just about every hot spot in Abu Dhabi and Dubai. Then I started to notice that the people around me, especially the older ones, were not growing or mature. I also realized most of the people in the community I hung around were fake, messy, and, again, not maturing. There were forty-year-olds sleeping with twenty-somethings and catching STDs like they were in their teens. There really wasn't a single person for me to look up to cause, like me at this moment, they were stuck in a cycle and at much older ages. You're just as good as the company you keep or the community you live in. So, one of the first decisions I made was to put in my resignation and go home. So, I'm in school, praying more, and making sound and logical decisions that would help change my life for the better. I am starting to feel like my old self a little bit more and more and just kind of getting better. Then one day, all hell broke loose again. I picked up the phone one day and talked to my mom as usual, and things turned. A big explosion happened, and it was so gross, devastating, and ridiculous and made it all the way to

Facebook. I was so over it at that point and so pissed off with my mother that between my sniffles, I realized that this was a cycle, a toxic cycle at that! I had pretty much forgiven and tried to get over everything we had gone through in the past. If you read the first half of this book, you know this was not easy or light stuff to get past. Not only did I try to forgive her, but I also allowed her back into my life and space, and she still never really was a mother to me. Most of the time, she called or talked to me about something pertaining to one of my sisters. I am in a foreign country, dying internally, and 90% of our conversations pertained to other people. Then on this day, she calls me with a raggedy family mess; not only does she call me with it, but she also shows her whole behind for the world to see. That was it; that was the straw that broke the camel's back. I told her that day, you handle it, and I blocked her and both of my sisters. That was July 2020, it is now July 2022, and my mother has just, for the first time, had a conversation with me earlier this month (I will talk about this more later). We had come so far just to be flung back into a space that we had, in my mind, conquered and were never going back to. Sadly, I was mistaken, but I was also getting off that roller coaster ride of destruction with them. I was choosing me at this point. You can't be better for others when you can't be better for yourself and doing the same things and expecting a different result is insanity. Thinking she would just grow and change without self-work was insane. Then a few months later, I had the same situation happen with my father. Here is a man that had been locked up since I was five, trying to talk crazy to me about a decision I was making and just was expressing to him why I was choosing this particular thing, and here he was trying to judge me and tell me what he thought was best for me, meanwhile I did not have to talk to him at all, and he was not even in the free world to grasp anything I was trying to say. This was not the first time in a few months that he and

I had found ourselves arguing about things I expressed to him. Feelings should not lead to arguments, especially with someone who hasn't been around enough or done enough to even have such a negative response. So, the block list he went to as well. My first time talking to him was in June this year. Then, I stopped talking to some people, just cold turkey, and left most, if not all, the group chats I was in. I needed a clear mind, a new mind, and healthy spaces, and they weren't serving me. I really only spent time with my roommate, one of my best friends, Cheyenne. There were a few other associates I talked to, but I had become somewhat and purposefully secluded. Healing takes separation and even sometimes isolation. Separation and Isolation are not the same. Separation is taking yourself from certain things and some types of things, but Isolation is a complete withdrawal from everything. Some periods of your healing require community. A HEALTHY community and I mean the people God has sent to you to do life with. For me, healthy and Godly (Corinthians 6: 14-15). I'm a Christian Woman (I may not always appear as one), and I require people in my life that know God, serve Him, love Him, and want Him with the same intensity as I do. So, when I am in a separation period, they are there as well, encouraging me, sharpening me, holding me accountable, praying for me, and pouring into me (Proverbs 27:17, Proverbs 18:24). Isolation is nobody but God and me, and that is usually during a fast. God did not make us to be alone and especially not for long (Romans 12:4-5). I had to learn that, unlike the average person, I thrive in isolation. I thrive in isolation because I have learned to be alone, not to trust anyone, and to make way for myself. I never really had too many people (I learned in therapy that I had a detachment disorder) I felt close to, and the people I did try to get close to would hurt me. They weren't the right people, and having the right people is much greater than having the wrong people or just anybody in your life for that matter. You can really do bad all by yourself.

11

Transitioning Part 1

On Dec 27, 2020, I flew home to Birmingham, AL, for good. I was officially done in the UAE, and in some ways, I immediately felt better. Being able to see and hug my grandmother, hold my nieces and nephew and just simply spend time around the ones I loved and not being on a time clock to leave was amazing. I needed that more than I ever knew, and God was about to raise up new relationships and bonds in my life now that I was somewhat settled. I started 2021 off with a fast. I usually fasted with my church at the beginning of the year for 21 days, and I committed to doing that. I know that this fast prepared me for the new things I would experience in 2021, fresh off the heels of two horrific years and still trying to restore myself from it. I really did not need any more experiences because I had been through enough, but that's the thing about life, you're always transitioning. Experience is what causes us to transition. It doesn't matter if it's an easy or stressful transition; you're constantly moving. If you are not transitioning, then that actually may not be a good thing. You may be caught in a cycle or just not moving at all. A cycle does not produce growth; instead, it has a hamster on a wheel effect, moving, going, and possibly running, but nowhere fast. I know because, as I said, I was on this wheel for two years straight, and two years may not seem like a lot, but I just think about what I lost or possibly could have achieved during those dead seasons. Think about it, but don't dwell on it too long, because our God is faithful and said in His word that He would restore all of the things we've lost (Joel 2:25, Deuteronomy 30:3). My only advice for transitioning or life, in general, is stay close to God. I fasted and was going on with my life, and then I got Covid. I was ok, with minor flu-like symptoms and terrible headaches, but fine; God had already prepared me and I knew He would heal me. Then I started talking to this girl, she was very insistent on dating me, but she was in the closet. Cool, but a weird space to be in, because she was actually using her in the closet M.O. to lie to me. I take lying to heart, and you can't come back from that with me. I was so angry with her and the way she tried to manipulate me. I stopped talking to her that day and demanded she drive me home from the out-of-state vacation we were on. I know y'all are wondering why this is important. Well, that situation was one of the first things that built a trusting relationship between my aunt and me. I was able to confide in her about this situation, and she confided in me about some things. That situation transitioned our relationship. I had moved in with my aunt when I came back to the states because I was going right back to traveling in my career. This was not the same aunt I had lived with before; we had not had a deep relationship like the aunt I had stayed with. These are my father's sisters, and through family strife, I did not grow up with them, and we were now learning and leaning on each other. I got over that situation real fast and kept pushing, still on my new journey and getting back acquainted in the USA. Things were going fine then I met this man. He was so nice and charming, and we clicked. He owned his own business and was free all the time, like me, and we went on dates for weeks almost every other day. We were good, and then I got a start date at my new job in New York, and from that day on, things changed. He first started to attack my independence (which he swore he loved because he was tired of needy women), spewing all of this Kevin Samuels rhetoric. Soon after having a few months of chaos, toxicity, and dealing with his narcissistic behaviors, I left. Before I left, though, I noticed that the peace I fought to get and the healing journey I was on was now somewhat thwarted. I had been so triggered throughout the relationship that I started to see old habits, feelings, and behaviors spring forth. I had just gone through an entire year of trying to escape these negative energies and decided I needed counseling. There was no way I was going back to what I just had gotten over. Most of my summer in New York in 2021 was spent in counseling. Our situation caused me to re-examine where I was and decide what was best for me. I needed further counseling anyway (I never finished counseling in Abu Dhabi), and this was just another way for God to gently push me on the road He had laid out for me. This is another example of what the enemy meant for evil... God does allow challenges to happen to shape our lives and futures (Romans 5:3-5). I just don't believe He causes the traumas. I thought I was fine with my prayers, watching church, fasting, talking with friends, and reading self-help books. I was, but still, there was a missing key. The things I had gone through really required professional help. I had been traumatized for most of my life, and that does something to you. It changes you and reprograms you into something and someone you may not even recognize or know what to do with yourself. This was definitely where I was, and God wanted to develop more out of me (Philemon 1:6). My therapist was an older black woman from the south who loved God. She was also a straight shooter that did not cut corners, so I instantly respected her. She was able to coach and love me through my trauma (she's a trauma specialist), but also held me accountable for sticking through my needed changes and development. My life changed that summer, and since then I have been at the greatest level of peace in my life, immovable peace. I know that I'm at that level because there have been many more issues since then that have tested me in many ways, and instead of my old ways, I can truly say I have been responding from a place of growth. I may have a slip, we're talking about a year and a slip or two (vs living in strife, fights, anger, and chaos almost daily), so I know that I have found control, and I am over the biggest hill on this journey and can confidently say that I have been healed, though the journey is never-ending. Things may trigger me, hurt me, and constantly come my way, but I know who my strength comes from, who I am, and whose I am, so my healing shall sustain, no matter what. I have the tools, and I shall continually do the work.

12

Restoration and New creature
Part 1 (1 Peter 5:10)

I was so happy about the restoration God was doing. I did not realize or understand that He was going to do more than that in my life. Restoration is just one level of healing, and I was extremely grateful; going about life not feeling like yourself is troublesome by itself. I literally was so bad off; I was dimming my shine. I remember a co-worker telling me she knew something was wrong with me but did not know what it was. She told me that whatever it was, was affecting her too. She told me she looked up to me, and if I wasn't strong and okay, she did not feel like she could make it either. That really struck me. Here I was used to being this strong, out loud, bold, resilient, and always smiling person that people really looked up to, confided in, and took strength from through my encouraging them; I had now, for those years, only been a picture of that, not truly the full embodiment of who I truly was. I cannot say I was fake because that was and is truly who I am, but I was not operating as Krystal Ashley Hughes, Queen, Krys, that girl, Queenkrys, Big Krys, HER, Miss Girl, the doll, Diamond in the sky, Kmoney, and whatever else people called me. God started restoring me from the moment I started praying and crying after hanging up from my aunt's friend. He restored my tongues. That was the first recognizable thing He gave me back. Then he restored my feelings, this was big because I cannot say I wanted them back, LOL. I was just used to being rough, numb, and saw feelings as a weakness. I had a hard time accepting this because, again, sensitivity grosses me out. Then He taught me through the third restoration, Trust, that having feelings was not a weakness but a necessary vulnerability that has so many benefits. The feelings helped me cry; in other words, they cleansed me. I used to be so angry at myself for crying, like pissed off and ready to fight. The thing about feelings/emotions is that accessing and expressing my feelings helped create more boundaries and demand more respect from anybody in or entering my life. Everyone always knew I was not one to play with, but this actually shows what my expectations are and how I operate. It actually has eased tensions and made people understand me better. Once you set the standard, the people God is directing into your life will accept and respect who you are without any opposition (Any opposition or too much opposition, ask yourself and God if they are really supposed to be in my life, we hold on to too many people out of familiarity and loyalty versus love, respect, and God Divine order). I also reciprocate people's needs and wants regarding their life, who they are, and my place in their life. Then there is trust. Trust was also another tricking one for me. Trust who? I literally had people in my life who were showing me their trustworthiness, and I could not even see it because I had been betrayed so many times (Y'all only read about one). I remember doing an exercise in counseling, and one of the books I had to fill in told me to list down five people I trust. It blew my mind. I had to think so hard and even second guess my answers. That let me know I was really bad off. I should have easily and confidently written down my grandmother, my two aunts, my sister directly under me, and my friend Chey. A few had made me question their trustworthiness before, but we had talked about it and mended it, and I knew I could trust them. I didn't write them immediately, though, because there was still this feeling deep inside of me that I just could not trust anybody. It still creeps up at times, but it has gotten a lot better, especially with some of the things I and those five, and a few others have gone through, have shared and been tested through. I now have a whole God-given community, and it's amazing. Then after trust came vulnerability, yes you guessed it, lol, another thing I had difficulty with. I have always been somewhat transparent but to a certain extent. I have always been my second and right-hand man; in other words, I and my self-consciousness are the only ones who knew and felt it all. I was just guarded about myself; by now, you see why, but God started teaching me to be vulnerable. There are only certain levels of healing you will reach if you lack vulnerability. There are only certain levels of God you will reach if you lack vulnerability. I stand on both of those previous statements because through my vulnerability; I have been able to see and feel the new levels unlock and the rise of the Holy Spirit deep within me. He literally told me to write this book through someone I was being vulnerable with. I had to get that message through her prophecy and probably would have never gotten it if I was never vulnerable enough to hear, receive, or talk things over with her (Another close friend Kameisha). The Bible also calls us to vulnerability (James 5:16); that is just one scripture, but there are so many where He tells us to have an open heart, talk to others, repent to others and walk in vulnerability. Vulnerability was a new thing in me, but He told me through my many prayer sessions with Him that I have personally or once a week with my good friend Naamonde, that He was making us new creatures, never before seen. If you have been close to me and know or heard many things I have turned my cheeks to, then you would already know how much of a new person He has created. There are so many things that I could have acted on, so many people I could have cursed out (my mouth is so lethal), and so many situations I could have meddled in but chose to be the bigger person. I am shocking myself because what 2021, 2020, 2019, 2018, and 2017 Krystal would have done or said would not have been anything nice. God has His hand on me, He has healed me, and He's further healing, transitioning, and creating me to be a new person. He can do the same for you! You don't have to lose yourself; it is literally some parts of me He is urging me to keep. What you do lose was never meant to be there in the first place, and it is most likely not serving you. Lose yourself in God and let Him purpose and prune you for His will in your life. There is where I am now in 2022, allowing Him to do all His works and wonders in my life by obeying and following His subtle commandments. I am not perfect, and pretty sure I will never be, but what I am is becoming the beautiful creature that God is using to get His glory and to bring others into His glory, and that's alright with me!

13

Let's recap my healing journey,
So that you may see it clearly
and Begin your own!

1 DO SOMETHING!

As I stated in the opening of this book, healing is active, not passive. You cannot just lay around all day and night and pray; God heal me, God heal me, and simply expect Him to do it. There are a lot of things that go into healing. Faith is the biggest of them all! You have to believe that you can make it out of your current situation and that He can deliver you, because He can! Also, you have to get real about yourself and others around you. If anybody can treat you any kind of way, they will! That is not okay from anybody; I told y'all earlier in this part of the book that I stopped speaking to my parents for two whole years. I'm not bragging about it, but I demanded respect and peace from them because we were literally going in circles, and if this doesn't get fixed now, this generational curse of brokenness will continue to manifest in more generations. I told them both I would never talk to them again unless it was in counseling. I am happy to report we are now in counseling and working through major issues. It is just the beginning, but it is going well, sometimes rocky, but overall good. I trust God to see it through. He said He will in Philippians 1:6. I do understand that it is difficult if you depend on someone or love them, but figure it out! Also, not everyone's situation is as bad as mine and my parent's situation. Judge your situation accordingly and pray for it. Remember, it's always You vs Everybody. You have to treat yourself well to make others treat you well. You are literally teaching people how to treat you by what you accept. Last thing, move, start a new job, get a new hobby, meet new people. Do whatever you need to do to refresh yourself and find your happiness. Your joy is more valuable than a high-paying job, a fake marriage, societal status, or anything else. Seek help, from the right sources, church, healthy friendships, counseling, YouTube sermons, etc. There are a bunch of ways to get the help you need. I do not want to hear the excuses. "Churches are full of hypocrites," many state, so you've been to every church in the world? The same way you are willing to give a new guy or girl a try after 5011 of them have been trash, you can do the same for the church. The church is your community of believers and backbone. Those devos and sermons helped me during the beginning of my journey. Pray about your friends; God will literally remove who is not for you and when He shows you who is not, leave them. Sometimes it is not who they are to you but their character as a whole. Leave them; God will send you brand new people; trust me, I know. I have lost so many people along the way, and not one of them is worth me making up with. The people that are/is, I have. Some people and situations are seasonal. As far as counseling, it is not a million dollars. Do not let anyone lie to you about that. My Better Help sessions on betterhelp.com were literally like $85, and I was on the higher end because I was considered well off, so I know it's much cheaper depending on where you fall financially. I am now doing private sessions, and they are $60 a week. I see people sell stamps for $150 Jordans or a wig; there are really no excuses. You are choosing whether to look better on the outside or do the work on the inside, and only one can really pay off. Materials are temporary and fleeting, lose value, can be stolen, tarnished, etc. YOU are once in a lifetime! Also, seek out community resources or job resources for therapy; they are out there! Hotlines are also available to talk to someone for free; I've called one. If you don't trust anybody else or God to save you, save yourself. You Matter! Therapy is a tool; with that tool, you have to be willing to do the work. I advise you not to waste your time, money, or a therapist's time if you are not willing to do the work to change. It will not be easy, but it will be worth it if you go and at least try. There are times you will have to look yourself in the mirror and say, yes, I did that, yes, that is me, and sometimes that will be hard. You will have to take accountability on your part and forgive yourself and be willing to grow. You have to be willing to go through the process of therapy and trust the process of therapy. It is not just a place to vent; it is a place to learn, grow and change. So many people are wasting their time in therapy because they are not willing to change or don't want to change.

2 Transitioning Part 2

Transitioning was probably the hardest part of my healing journey. I was so tired of going from this to that and back again. I was like, I need a break, but transitions are the only way to get from glory to glory—the only way to learn, grow, and get to purpose. Pastor Toure Roberts said on one of his podcasts that he went through nineteen transitions in twenty two years. Yes, I had the same reaction; what? I am tired! He went on to speak on how transitions were going to be forever present in our lives, and that is exactly what I explained to you guys in this chapter. I would rather be put through the tests and challenges of life every day than to be seated, not moving, not changing, and not evolving. That is kind of like the fifty-year-old in a full Jordan outfit at the club, trying to talk to all the twenty-year-olds because that is where his mindset is stuck. So, I have learned to embrace it and even the bad things that life has brought. The Bible tells us to count it ALL joy (James 1:2)! Joy is what you have despite the chaos, challenges, and drama. It is what keeps you going and the reason many of us do not look like what we have been through. I meet people and sometimes tell them about my story, and the first thing they say is, I would have never guessed any of that was your life. I still smile, dress my tail off, dance, travel, and live my best life in every way possible. Joy is what was taken from me two years ago, and now I have gotten it back and also gained its sister, Peace.

3 Restoration and New Creature Part 2

Restoring yourself is as simple as doing your hair, cleaning, posting pictures, and going out to eat again. I went through a period where I hated how I looked, and I did not want to be considered pretty or beautiful anymore. The way men kept approaching me and making advances at me had me questioning every picture I posted or would not post at all. Then I started to see that men were still approaching me this way even when I was covered. It was not me; it was them, and a lot of people are truly sick. No matter how covered I am, my face card never declines, and unless I start wearing the older school hijabs (the ones with only the eyes showing), I will always be looked at or approached by men. That arose from my rape and the unwanted sexual advances from different men. It was up to me to fight through that and get back to posting like I used to. Those are all small ways to start restoring yourself; through God, He will restore you in a deeper, spiritual way. He is the molder and will restore and shape you for His purposes (Jeremiah 18:1-6). As far as becoming a New Creature, I say you can determine how that looks in your life as well, or at least start it and let God finish it. You can change how you dress; you can change how you talk, where you go, what you do, and even what you eat. God gave us free will, so with that comes choices and certain choices help to propel us. Being active in the gym can keep you fit and fine. Going back to school can increase your financial situation or give you the feeling of accomplishment you may need. Even as small as going on a hike in a different direction than you normally do can be the new change you need. Who knows what you have yet to discover on that path? God also promises a new life and new things (Isaiah 43:18-19). Trust that He will do it!

14

THE END

If you made it this far, I want to first say Thank You for reading! God is amazing, and He chose me to deliver this message to you. This is my story, but it is all for HIS Glory. I truly believe that what He did and is doing for me, He can do for you as well if you seek Him, trust Him, and believe in Him. If you look at my socials or my past, you will see I am not the model Christian that the world has told us we had to be and act like to be loved or used by Him. Do I think I can be better? Absolutely, God and I are working on that daily. Should you or I sit in shame because we fell short or aren't perfect? Nope, but we should strive to get it right and hold ourselves accountable. God is the only person who can change us deeply trust me I know. When you say you want to change and commit to Him, He will definitely convict you. He will literally bother me until I turn around and do what He says or correct my mistakes. I rarely let it get to that these days, though, because I want to obey Him; I crave to.

Allow me to introduce myself, My name is Krystal A. Hughes, I was born and raised in Birmingham, AL and now currently living in Atlanta, GA. I am 33 years young at the time of publishing this book. My hobbies include, everything, lol, no really everything: traveling (30+ countries and counting), skating, biking, working out, dancing, reading, watching documentaries and so many other things. If you would like to keep up with me, my adventures, or my life journey, you can follow me on FB: Krystal A. Hughes, IG: krys.hughes and for more info or opportunities email me at readmystoryheargodsglory@gmail.com

Tre Hazelwoood

www.ingramcontent.com/pod-product-compliance
Lightning Source LLC
Chambersburg PA
CBHW060349130626
46553CB00003B/1151